CLOSE-UP
A Focus on Nature

SILVER BURDETT PRESS

© 1995 Silver Burdett Press
Published by Silver Burdett Press.
A Simon & Schuster Company
299 Jefferson Road, Parsippany, NJ 07054
Printed in the United States of America

Library of Congress
Cataloging-in-Publication Data
Gohier, François.
    Humpback whales: traveling on the wings of a
song/by François Gohier; photographs by François
Gohier.
        p. cm.--(Close up)
    ISBN 0-382-24887-2 (LSB)   10 9 8 7 6 5 4 3 2 1
    ISBN 0-382-24888-0 (SC)   10 9 8 7 6 5 4 3 2
    1. Humpback whale--Juvenile literature.
[1. Humpback whale. 2. Whales.] I. Title.
II. Series: Close up (Parsippany, N.J.)
QL737.C424G63 1994   94-30907
599.5'1--dc20   CIP
                                               AC

HUMPBACK WHALES

Writer and Photographer
François Gohier

Series Editor
Vicki León

Designers
David Butz and Ashala Nicols-Lawler

SILVER BURDETT PRESS

© 1995 Silver Burdett Press
Published by Silver Burdett Press.
A Simon & Schuster Company
299 Jefferson Road,
Parsippany, NJ 07054
Printed in the United States of America

The sea is full of strange music. But no vocalization is more haunting or complex than the song of the humpback whale. Like a bird song, it uses musical building blocks called units and phrases to build complex themes that are repeated in a certain order. Rhythmic in nature, humpback songs even contain a surfacing theme, sung when the whale comes up to breathe. Below and on pages 5, 17, and 36 of this book you'll see three themes from a humpback's musical "score." Although researchers have heard humpbacks make feeding and social sounds, including interactions between mothers and calves, they believe that only males sing. So the long, eerie melodies of the deep may be songs of courtship.

2.0
1.5
1.0
.5
KHz 0
0 1 2 3 4 5 6 7 8 9 10 11 12 13 14 15 16 17 18 19
SECONDS

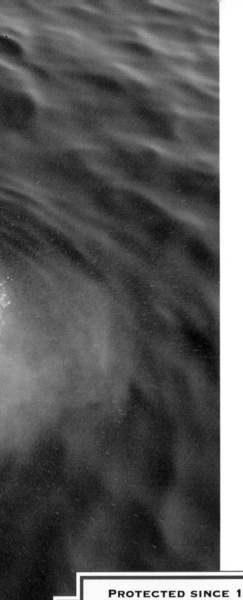

GENTLE AND CURIOUS SINGER OF SONGS

O f all the whales in the sea, the humpback may be the most beloved. As whales go, it's an unhandsome creature, chunky rather than sleek in shape and warty as a pickle. Perhaps we delight in the humpback because of its behavior. As 19th-century writer Herman Melville wrote in his famous novel, *Moby Dick*: "The Hump Back is the most gamesome and light-hearted of all whales, making more gay foam and white water generally than any other of them."

In Melville's time, little was known of the great baleen whales. From his experience at sea on whaling vessels, Melville hinted at what makes the humpback so attractive to modern whale watchers: its remarkable aptitude for aerial display. Scientists today shy away from words like "light-hearted" to describe a humpback's actions. They argue that breaching, flipper slapping, and other spectacular behaviors have a social function or a survival value and should not be considered as play. In young calves, however, the idea of true play is now widely accepted.

In the 1960s, researchers discovered that humpbacks sing. Recordings of these long, eerie melodies have been

PROTECTED SINCE 1966 FROM HUMAN HUNTING, HUMPBACKS MAY NUMBER ONLY 10,000 TO 12,000 ANIMALS. EVEN THOUGH BOATS ARE NOT ALLOWED TO GET CLOSE, WHALE-WATCHING OFF NORTH AMERICA IS VERY POPULAR. FROM TIME TO TIME, AS HERE IN NEW ENGLAND, CURIOUS WHALES GIVE LUCKY VIEWERS A THRILL BY APPROACHING THE BOATS OF THEIR OWN ACCORD.

widely broadcast, another factor which has given humpbacks a special place in the public's heart.

For the past two decades, the behaviors and songs of the humpbacks have been intensely studied. The coastal nature of the species has also made it possible for many thousands of adults and children to see whales in their natural habitat. While usually slow and placid, humpbacks sometimes live up to their gamesome reputations, rewarding us with some of the most exhilarating displays in the animal world.

Like all whales and dolphins, humpbacks are mammals. They give birth to live young and have mammary glands. In their first months, the young live solely on mother's milk. Whales have lungs and breathe air. Some 65 million years ago, their distant ancestors were small land mammals that slowly adapted to life in the sea. After the Age of the dinosaurs, the great predatory marine reptiles also vanished. Food became plentiful in the marine environment, and mammals moved to occupy it. They evolved into many different forms, some of which are now extinct. Today there are eleven species of baleen whales and 68 of toothed whales, collectively called "cetaceans."

One of them, the blue whale, became the largest animal ever to have lived on

AN AIR BREATHER, THE HUMPBACK NEEDS TO COME TO THE SURFACE AT REGULAR INTERVALS. THE HUMPBACK EJECTS ITS SPOUT OR BLOW FROM A PAIR OF BLOWHOLES OR NOSTRILS FOUND ON TOP OF ITS LONG BUMPY HEAD.

Can you hum along with the humpbacks? Below is theme A from the musical score of a whale song. Its highs, lows, and rhythms are punctuated with rests, just as human music is. Humpback males can send their mighty songs across five miles of ocean.

earth, bigger than any dinosaur yet discovered. Although they would dwarf a sailboat or a truck, humpbacks are smaller than blues. Averaging 45 feet in length, adults weigh about 25 tons. Females tend to be slightly larger than males. Humpbacks have wide heads and stocky bodies that taper to a muscular tail stock called the caudal peduncle. Their 10- to 12-foot-wide tails or flukes make a deep "V" in the middle and have serrated edges. Like other whales, the flukes propel the humpback with powerful upward and downward strokes.

You can most easily recognize a humpback by spotting its long, flexible flippers or pectoral fins. They extend almost one-third of the length of the body – longer than any other whale's fins. The Latin name of the species, *Megaptera novaeangliae*, means "big-winged New Englander," and refers to these extravagant fins and to the area where the species has most recently been scientifically described.

What does the common name "humpback" refer to? Two-thirds of the way down the body, you can see a well-defined fatty dorsal fin, which varies in shape from rather square to triangular. When the whale dives, it also arches its tail stock at a sharp angle. The whalers called it the "Hump Back" for both these reasons.

In the northern hemisphere, humpbacks are black on the top and sides of the body, while the underpart is partially – sometimes entirely – white. Southern hemisphere animals, in Australia, for example, have much more white, sometimes running up the sides of the body.

Flippers vary greatly too. Animals off the east coast

HUMPBACKS MAY LOOK ALIKE TO US, BUT THEY HAVE SOMETHING AS USEFUL AS FINGERPRINTS TO TELL ONE FROM ANOTHER. EACH TAIL FLUKE DISPLAYS A PATTERN AS UNIQUE AS A SNOWFLAKE, WHICH CAN BE PHOTOGRAPHED FOR RESEARCH. THEY USE THEIR TAILS TO LOB OR SLAP THE WATER, SOMETIMES IN APPARENT AGGRESSION.

of North America tend to have completely white flippers. Pacific Coast humpbacks are usually darker on the dorsal surface, but you may also find whales with bright white flippers in the Pacific.

Besides being wide, the head of a humpback is long: about one-third of its total length. Both jaws are lined with a series of large, warty-looking bumps, called knobs or tubercles. The whalers used to call them "stove bolts," and joked that they held the head of the whale together. Each of these bumps supports a single hair, which attaches to a half-inch cluster of nerves. These hair follicles are sensory organs which have been compared to a cat's whiskers. They probably allow the whale to detect small movements or vibrations in

THE GREAT STRENGTH AND AGILITY OF A HUMPBACK BECOMES APPARENT WHEN IT TAIL BREACHES, BRINGING ITS TAIL STOCK AND FLUKES UP OUT OF THE WATER AND SMASHING VIOLENTLY SIDEWAYS IN AN EXPLOSIVE DISPLAY. DURING COURTSHIP BATTLES, MALES EVEN HIT EACH OTHER WITH THEIR TAILS.

the water, perhaps caused by another whale nearby or by the small fishes and krill that make up the humpback's diet.

Humpbacks have up to 30 well-marked throat grooves running from chin to navel. They help the throat expand like a purse.

That lets the humpback maximize the volume of sea water and food taken in a single lunge.

On the top of the head are the nostrils or twin blowholes through which the humpback breathes. In front of them sits a ridge called the splash-guard, which helps prevent water from entering the blowholes as the whale surfaces. The humpback's blowholes are very sensitive and flexible. The whale may be able to control them as finely as we can control our own lips. The humpback can open these nostrils just enough to release a delicate stream of bubbles, and can increase the size of the opening at will.

It can also control the shape of the opening, in combination with the pressure of the expelled air, to produce sounds. The normal exhale sound of a humpback is a long, deep "pfoouuuh..." followed by the brief, whistling sound of its inhalation. When excited, humpbacks often emit a sharp, loud call called a "trumpet blow."

Often the first – or only – sign we see of a whale is its blow or spout. Why is the blow visible? Because of the condensation of the moisture contained in the warm air expelled under great pressure. And because the sea water remaining on top of the blowholes at the instant of their opening is atomized and mixed with the blow itself. With humpbacks, the spout is bushy and pear-shaped. After a long dive, when the whale exhales with great strength, the blow can also be narrow, straight, and 15 to 20 feet tall. In the cold, still atmosphere of Alaska, these white columns can hang in the air for some time after the whale has disappeared beneath the surface.

Scientists think that 80% to 90% of the air in a whale's lungs is exchanged with

each breath, compared to 15% to 20% for us. The whales need to store enough oxygen for the time they spend underwater. Even so, humpbacks need to come up for air at regular intervals.

Humpbacks are found around the world, but are not randomly distributed throughout the oceans. They summer in cold, high-latitude waters and winter in the tropics. Because the seasons are reversed in the northern and southern hemispheres, the northern and southern populations of humpbacks never meet. When it is summer in the Arctic north, and the whales are in the polar region, it is winter in

the south and the southern whales are in the tropics. Six months later, the situation is reversed. By the time the northern whales reach the tropics, the southern humpbacks have moved towards Antarctica.

The different humpback populations we know today may have come from a common ancestral group that lived around the Antarctic. From there, the animals colonized the oceans of the world. Because of the present world climate and configuration of the continents, these populations are now isolated from one another and do not interbreed. They are slowly diverging; this helps explains some of the differences between groups.

Unlike gray whales, which migrate close to shore and in relatively shallow waters, humpbacks cross vast expanses of open ocean. For weeks they travel, probably moving over depths that measure thousands of feet and meeting currents that vary in speed and direction.

Yet the whales that leave their summer feeding grounds in the Gulf of Alaska manage to reach their goal: the Hawaiian Islands, tiny dots isolated in the greatest ocean on earth. How they navigate so surely is not certain. One promising theory argues that humpbacks may use the earth's magnetic field to orient themselves. Magnetite, a metalloid substance found in humpback brains, might enable them to find their way.

A calf could learn the migration path from its mother; current research supports this hypothesis. Humpbacks have a great fidelity for their feeding areas, the same individuals returning to the same sites year after year. Individually identified calves swimming with their mothers to feeding grounds have also been seen to return to the same place on their own in subsequent years.

As the whales leave the polar latitudes with the onset of winter, they face another difficulty: how to find one another to mate. Once in the tropics, they tend to congregate in bays and shallow waters around islands. Groups that feed in distinct areas meet and intermingle on the breeding grounds. In the Atlantic, for example, humpbacks feeding in

DURING COURTSHIP, VARIOUS MALES FIGHT OVER ONE FEMALE. IN THE PROCESS, THEY MAY INFLICT WOUNDS ON EACH OTHER. DNA TESTING SHOWS THAT CALVES FROM ONE FEMALE HAVE DIFFERENT FATHERS. CLEARLY, HUMPBACKS DON'T MATE FOR LIFE.

the Gulf of Maine, and off Newfoundland, Greenland, and Iceland, all gather in the Caribbean. In the Pacific, humpbacks from Central California go to Mexico, while animals feeding in Southeast Alaska and Prince William Sound go to Hawaiian waters.

But things are not always cut and dried in the humpback's world. It is now believed that a few animals in the Pacific occasionally change their winter destination, sometimes going towards Mexico instead of Hawaii, and vice-versa. Some whales may even travel along much more complex routes. In 1986, for example, a humpback that had been observed at Isla Socorro, off the coast of Mexico, was seen again in Hawaii, six weeks and about 3,000 miles later. We don't know how the humpbacks solve the navigational problems involved in such journeys, but their ability to do so is indeed very impressive.

Slow and graceful, humpbacks are aware and at home in their environment. Because they calmly avoid human divers, people call them "gentle giants." Giants they are, and gentle too, most of the time. During the breeding season, however, competition for access to females leads the males into fierce and bloody battles. Ironically, courting begins with a song.

The songs of humpbacks have been heard for thousands of years by sailors and voyagers. Even at the beginning of our modern era, no one knew what in the sea was responsible for these strange melodies. In the 1950s, people working with the U.S.

Navy recorded these sounds, noting they were heard only during the season when humpbacks were present. Subsequent research showed that the sounds were organized in ways that warranted calling them "songs." Longtime researcher Jeff Jacobsen describes their ponderously rhythmic, almost hypnotic quality for us here. "The grunts, screams, roars, and trumpeting sounds the humpbacks make are organized in a specific, repetitive order, first observed by Roger and Katharine Payne and their associates. Each individual stereotyped sound the whale

> NEWBORN CALVES STAY CLOSE TO MOTHERS. THIS CALF, ABOUT ONE WEEK OLD, WEIGHS OVER A TON. IN ONE YEAR, IT WILL NEARLY DOUBLE ITS LENGTH. NURSING TAKES PLACE AT THE MAMMARY SLITS ON THE MOTHER'S UNDERSIDE. THERE, THE CALF GETS THICK, RICH MILK SQUIRTED INTO ITS MOUTH. WHILE TRAVELING, THE YOUNG CALF OFTEN SWIMS ABOVE AND TO ONE SIDE OF ITS MOTHER'S HEAD, AS YOU SEE AT RIGHT.

makes is called a unit. A unit may be sung once, or repeated many times in a row, separated by brief moments of silence. Usually a series of three or four different units is sung in a specific order, called a phrase. Generally a humpback repeats a phrase numerous times to make a theme. Then the singer begins a new phrase,

composed of units which are usually different from those of the first phrase. The second phrase is repeated several times, forming a second theme. An average song lasts about 12 minutes. It may contain three to five themes, almost always sung in order. In a typical song session, the humpback will sing its song over and over for hours on end."

These are the basic things that have been discovered about humpback's songs in the world's oceans. Only males have been shown to sing, and they do it mostly during the breeding season. All males sing the same song. During the season, the song progressively changes, and all of the males sing the same changes.

The song sung at the beginning of the breeding season is different from the song at the end of it. The following year, the whales start with the new version. So the song you hear at any given moment can only be heard for a week or so, and then it is changed forever."

"North Atlantic humpbacks have a completely distinct song from North Pacific humpbacks because they are geographically isolated. Humpbacks from the southern hemisphere sing a different song than their northern cousins because their breeding and singing seasons are six months apart."

To record humpback songs, researchers use sensitive underwater hydrophones. But the sound is often so powerful it can be heard without the use of any equipment. During one of our photographic expeditions to the humpback breeding grounds off Mexico, we happened to be so close to singers that we could hear them above water. With the outboard engine turned off, many of the subtleties of the song were audible. Travelers spending the night in coves along the coast told us that they could hear the song of the whales right through the hulls of their sailboats!

Humpbacks adopt a peculiar position for singing: they hang head down in some 60 feet of water, their flippers moving slowly to help them maintain this position. Under good conditions, the song travels four to five miles underwater. It certainly must be a form of communication, but its exact role remains a mystery. Since it is heard mostly during the breeding season, it may be an important part of the courtship – possibly a way for males to attract the attention of females. More research may eventually give us better answers to these questions. Meanwhile, the haunting songs continue to fascinate not only other humpbacks in the sea, but many human beings as well.

The choice of a mate belongs to the female. But the chosen male, called "the primary escort" by researchers, usually has to fend off a number of challengers. As the male/female pair swims along, it is joined by other males, sometimes as many as 20. Then the battles begin in earnest. These aggressive groups are easily spotted at a great distance, even from the shore.

The males all joust for position near the female. They try to push each other away, ramming one another, and hitting the other whale with violent strokes of their tail flukes. They emit threatening bubble trails. They even inflate their throats to appear bigger as they throw themselves in powerful lunges towards their adversaries. Humpbacks seem to use

OVER A MILLION PEOPLE PER YEAR NOW WATCH WHALES, IT'S SAID. BECAUSE WHALE-WATCHING FOR HUMPBACKS CONTINUES TO GROW IN POPULARITY, IT'S IMPORTANT TO PROTECT THE ANIMALS FROM HARASSMENT. BOATS AND HUMANS MUST MAINTAIN A CERTAIN DISTANCE FROM WHALES TO KEEP THEM FREE OF STRESS. IF, HOWEVER, THE ANIMAL CHOOSES TO COME NEAR, WHALE-WATCHERS GET A RARE OPPORTUNITY TO SEE ONE OF THE GREAT WHALES OF THE OCEAN. ALONG BOTH COASTS OF NORTH AMERICA, HUMPBACKS OFTEN DELIGHT HUMANS WITH ENERGETIC AERIAL DISPLAYS. IT MAY NOT BE SCIENTIFIC, BUT THE FUN THEY SEEM TO BE HAVING IS CONTAGIOUS.

the sharp edge of the barnacles that grow on their throats and on the leading edge of their pectoral fins to cut each other's skin and make the opponent bleed. Scars from these courtship battles can be seen on many males.

Eventually, weaker males drop from the scene. In most fights, the animal that started as escort remains the escort. Current research indicates that this male may be the only one to mate with that particular female during a given season, but for that season only. By analyzing the DNA of a mother whale and several of her offspring, a technique called DNA fingerprinting has shown that successive calves have different fathers. In other words, despite popular belief, humpback whales do not mate for life.

No human has seen humpbacks mating. Exactly how and where it takes place remains yet another enigma. But there is no doubt that it occurs in tropical waters where, the following year, the calves will be born.

The mother who is about to give birth seeks out a protected cove. There, in calm water, the calf is born, probably tail first. The mother may help it to the surface for the first breath. On a few occasions, observers have seen calves that appeared to be lifted up by the mother's snout. It is hard to know if this was the mother's way of helping the newborn infant get its first breath, or if it was simply part of the close and complex relationship between mother and calf, which involves much nuzzling and touching.

If undisturbed, the mother humpback will stay with her baby in the same cove for

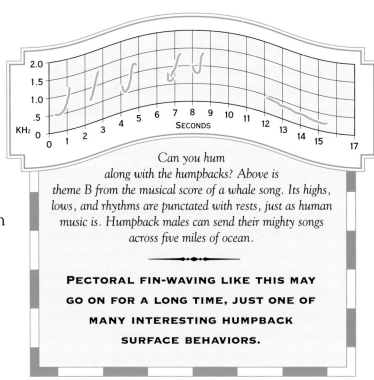

Can you hum along with the humpbacks? Above is theme B from the musical score of a whale song. Its highs, lows, and rhythms are punctated with rests, just as human music is. Humpback males can send their mighty songs across five miles of ocean.

PECTORAL FIN-WAVING LIKE THIS MAY GO ON FOR A LONG TIME, JUST ONE OF MANY INTERESTING HUMPBACK SURFACE BEHAVIORS.

several days. When I was photographing the humpbacks at Isla Socorro with a team of Mexican researchers, I had several opportunities to observe the behavior of mothers with very young calves. Typically, the female spent most of her time resting on the sand bottom in 60 to 80 feet of water, coming up to breathe every 15 to 20 minutes. The calf would come up more often at 3- to 5-minute intervals. It circled at the surface, taking several breaths, diving almost vertically to rejoin its mother.

Once I saw a calf spiraling down to the bottom where its mother was lying. It positioned itself at right angles to the mother's body, its head under the genital area where the nipples are located. There it stayed for a few seconds, then moved away to resume swimming over and around its mother's head. Although I saw no spilled milk or other evidence, this probably was a nursing bout. Humpback milk is very thick,

with a fat content of about 50%. The milk of humans and land mammals contains from 2% to 17% fat. The calf doesn't actually suck on the nipple; it positions its mouth against it, and the mother squirts in the milk.

About 12 feet long at birth, and weighing around one ton, the calf doubles its length in a year. Born in January or February, it stays with its mother for ten to 11 months. It swims with her to the summer feeding area, where it continues to nurse and probably learns to find its own food as well.

During the summer months, the calf slowly increases its time and distance away from its mother. The final separation usually occurs late in the year. Researchers have seen at least one calf separate from its mother at the feeding grounds, before the migration. More often, it happens during the migration or even when the animals are back in the tropics.

The female is probably alone when the baby is born. Sometimes another whale – usually an adult male – is seen with a cow and calf pair. The exact role of this male escort is unknown. It has been suggested that he may be there in the hope that the female will give him an opportunity to mate. While most females have calves at intervals of two or three years, some have been documented as having babies in consecutive years.

Sometimes the escort seems content just to keep the mother company, and rests as much as she does. I once saw such a group. The three animals were spending most of their time on the bottom, seldom coming up. When the dark shapes rose to the surface to breathe, I could easily recognize the escort. The tip of his left fluke was missing, bitten off by a killer whale. (We could tell this by the tooth marks on the rest of the tail.)

A few days later, we saw this animal again. He was then part of an active courting group. But our third encounter was the most memorable. The male was escorting yet

BREACHING IS THE MOST SPECTACULAR AERIAL DISPLAY OF THE HUMPBACK. WHEN THESE 25-TON MAMMALS EXPLODE OUT OF THE SEA, THE WATER RUNS DOWN THEIR PLEATED BODIES IN A QUICKSILVER PATTERN, ADDING TO THE BEAUTY AND EXCITEMENT. AFTER A BREACH, HUMP-BACKS USUALLY TRY TO FALL ONTO THEIR BACKS. ON PAGES 22-23, YOU CAN SEE ANOTHER BREACH BY A CALF.

LOTS OF WORK TO MAKE A MOUTHFUL: HUMPBACK WHALES USE A HUGE TONGUE TO STRAIN MASSES OF SHRIMP-LIKE KRILL, FISHES, AND SEAWATER THROUGH BRISTLY FILTERS CALLED BALEEN.

another mother and calf. This time, he was engaged in a highly acrobatic and thrilling aerial display: rolling, breaching, slapping his flippers, and more. Every now and then, the calf would become excited too. It would try to execute the same maneuvers, agitating its tiny flippers in the air while lying on its mother's back, or jumping halfway out of the water. The calf was clearly stimulated, and busy learning the behaviors that are so characteristic of humpback whales.

Why do humpback whales breach or leap out of the water, anyway? Why do they slap their flippers on the surface or turn themselves upside-down in the water to extend their tails and lob them sharply back and forth? Human speculation about these humpback behaviors is intense. As noted earlier, it's now been well accepted among biologists that young calves do these things as play. Many researchers, especially those working in Southeast Alaska, believe that the surface displays made by *adult* whales are territorial or stress statements.

The major difficulty we encounter in studying humpbacks is the obvious fact that they spend most of their time underwater. What triggers their behavior may very well elude us on most occasions. Another difficulty is that humpbacks leap in a great variety of contexts. This tells us there is more than one explanation for one type of action. For the present, let's look at some of the circumstances surrounding certain above-water behaviors.

A humpback may breach when meeting other whales. It may also breach when a pod splits into smaller groups. Or even when there is not another whale or boat in sight for miles around.

Whales may breach just once or many times over; humpbacks have been seen to breach more than 100 times in a row!

I have also seen long, complex sequences of behaviors. For instance, one whale began with a series of lob-tails,

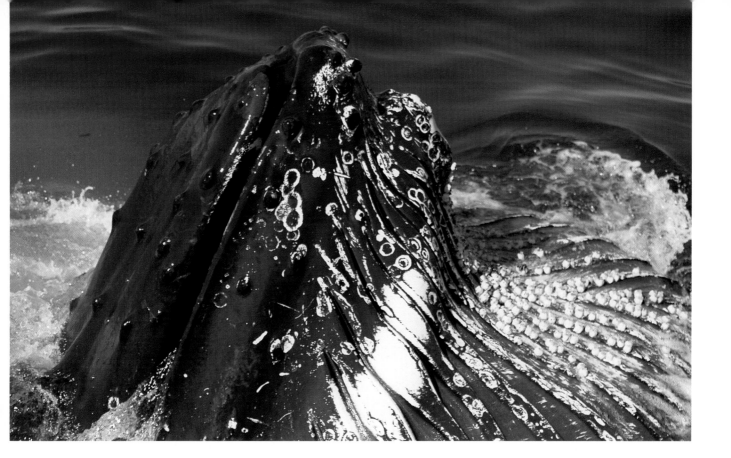

smacking its huge tail up and down on the surface while its body was head-down vertically under the water. The animal then righted itself, rolled up to breathe, then rolled on its side and slapped the water with one of its flippers, then the other one, occasionally rolling belly up and extending both flippers. It followed this with a long series of breaches, some of them taking this huge animal nearly out of the water.

Such displays can last an hour or more.

> WHILE FEEDING, HUMPBACKS OFTEN COME UP WITH MOUTHS AGAPE. IN AN UNUSUAL VARIATION, THE WHALE AT LEFT COMES UP SLOWLY, THEN DESCENDS WHILE SUCKING FISH INTO ITS MOUTH. HUMPBACKS ALSO HAVE BARNACLE-COVERED THROAT PLEATS THAT EXPAND, ALLOWING THEM TO TAKE IN ENORMOUS QUANTITIES OF SEAWATER AND FISHES AT A TIME.

I have seen them done by an escort and also by one whale in a pod of two. The second whale sometimes joined the other, the two of them making several perfectly synchronized double breaches. But I've also seen a lone humpback go through a long and complex sequence by itself.

Humpback whales not only feed and leap on the surface, they also sleep. Lying motionless with their flippers hanging at an angle to their bodies, they look much like logs. Like all cetaceans, humpbacks need to sleep in a half-alert state to regulate their breathing. As air breathers, they must make sure they only open their blowholes above the surface.

Each spring, the humpbacks of the northern hemisphere begin to leave the breeding area and swim thousands of miles north. Some animals arrive as early as April and begin to feed. The mothers and calves

are among the last to arrive. They stay longer in the warmer waters to allow the calf to grow and gain strength.

By late May or early June, all the whales have arrived in Alaska and the North Atlantic. In these food-rich waters, the sun has triggered a blossoming of tiny algae plants or phytoplankton, followed by microscopic animals or zooplankton. Both are being gobbled by the next creatures up the food chain, crustaceans and small fishes. These populations of krill, herring, capelin, and sand-lance explode. The humpbacks haven't fed since they went south the previous year, having lived on their blubber. Now it's time to gain back the tons they have lost. The hungry animals lunge through the schools of prey. Pleats in their throats allow them to take in

MORE THAN OTHER WHALES, HUMPBACKS USE A RANGE OF INGENIOUS TECHNIQUES TO FEED. THEY OFTEN COOPERATE, HERDING OR DISORIENTING THEIR PREY FOR BETTER RESULTS. IN ALASKA, THESE FEEDING GROUPS CAN NUMBER UP TO 20 WHALES.

huge volumes of sea water and food. Coming to the surface, the whale closes its mouth and contracts its throat. It expells the water through the brushy baleen filter inside its mouth, swallows, then dives again.

Humpbacks have developed several extraordinary feeding techniques. In lunge feeding, they lunge forward through a patch of food and gulp up enormous mouthsful. They have also learned how to herd their prey, concentrating it in the water to make the lunge more efficient.

The most amazing technique is called bubble netting, first studied and described by Dr. Charles Jurasz in Southeast Alaska in 1972. Once a school of fish has been located, the whale swims upwards while releasing air through its blowholes. The air

Bubble net feeding, pictured above, and lunge feeding, pictured at right,
are two of myriad techniques employed by the humpback. Like blue, minke, and fin whales, humpbacks are toothless filter feeders. They eat small schooling fishes and several varieties of krill, a tiny shrimp- or lobster-like crustacean. When conditions are right, krill form vast superswarms, up to a mile wide. Most humpback prey lives at a depth of 300 feet or less. That's why feeding takes place on or near the surface.

bubbles rise towards the surface, forming noisy, greenish columns that disorient the prey. The instinctive reaction of the fish is to tighten their formation, each fish trying to hide in the middle of the school, until they form a dense mass trapped within this bubble net. The whale appears at the surface, mouth open, and engulfs the water now boiling with food.

Bubble nets vary. A net can range in diameter from five to 150 feet. It can be made by one whale or several working together. Nets can consist of bubbles as small as pearls, released in a delicate stream, or of bubbles as big as basketballs. It can resemble a fine continuous curtain or look like huge columns almost evenly spaced. On the surface, bubble nets can appear as a circle, a spiral, or if incomplete, an arc.

Bubble netting is the technique of choice for Alaskan whales. Some New England animals use it too, but most prefer a variant known as bubble cloud. The whale releases a huge volume of air at once, and this seems to

accomplish the same thing. The fishes close rank and try to escape but are trapped beneath the surface where the whale, rising with open mouth through the cloud of bubbling water, catches up with them.

Cooperative feeding is another ploy. Groups of up to a dozen or more work together repeatedly. The whales concentrate the fish and come up together at the surface. They may seem to be bumping into each other randomly, but observers have proven that the same animals always occupy the same position within the group.

A humpback can eat more than a ton of food a day. Through the summer, the whales exploit an area, moving back and

Whales and humans sometimes fish together. In Alaska, salmon boats work while humpbacks feed in the cold, nutrient-rich waters.

forth in search of huge concentrations of fishes and crustaceans. Alternately feeding, resting, and socializing, the humpbacks stay in the north until the fall. Then they return to their breeding areas. Or most of them do. In Southeast Alaska, some animals stay year-round. They spend the winter in the straits and sounds between the area's many islands. Fishermen sometimes see them there. Short

days and cold weather make it difficult for biologists to study them at this time, however.

In the last century, whalers hunted humpbacks as they did other baleen species. We now guess their worldwide population to be about 10,000 to 12,000 individuals, down from perhaps 100,000 originally. In 1966, humpbacks came under worldwide protection. Since 1986, there has been a moratorium on whaling of any species, mocked by a few countries but honored by most nations.

The whaling years gave us knowledge of humpback anatomy, their parasites and diseases, and their seasonal distribution. Modern science, however, has given us the greatest insights into the life of these animals. Observing them in their natural environment without killing them or interfering

> **TAIL LOBBING IS ANOTHER SPECIAL BEHAVIOR IN THE SURFACE-ACTIVE REPERTOIRE OF THE HUMPBACK. THE ANIMAL GETS INTO A VERTICAL UPSIDE-DOWN POSITION, THEN REARS ITS TAIL INTO THE AIR. AT LEFT, A KILLER WHALE HAS LEFT TOOTH MARKS ON THE FLUKES OF THE WHALE.**

with their activities has allowed us to learn a great deal more than slaughtering them.

The key to detailed studies is to be able to recognize individual whales. This became possible in 1967 when it was proven that the underside of the humpback's tail flukes has permanent patterns as unique to each whale as fingerprints are to us. Dr. Charles Jurasz pioneered this technique

HUMPBACKS MAY LIVE 30 TO 60 YEARS. CALVES, SUCH AS THIS ONE PLAYING IN THE FEEDING GROUNDS OF ALASKA, REMAIN WITH MOTHERS FOR A YEAR OR SO. IT'S GENERALLY AGREED THAT HUMPBACK CALVES LOVE TO PLAY. THEY MAY SPEND HOURS ROLLING, JUMPING, AND LEARNING ADULT BEHAVIORS.

in Alaska. Since then, researchers the world over have used this method, photographing the animals and cataloging them. Thousands of photos have now been entered onto a computer data base.

Resightings can now give us a wealth of data on sexual maturity, birth rate, lifespan, social interactions, migration, and other important study subjects. In both Alaska and New England, some whales have been tracked through several generations, and will continue to be studied by future generations of biologists.

In the late 1970s, people other than scientists and fishermen got an opportunity to see whales in the wild. The whale-watching charter industry blossomed, making it possible and fun for anyone who is curious about whales to meet them in their environment. Humpbacks, which are quite surface oriented and have a propensity for aerial display, are favorite and rewarding subjects.

No amount of reading or video-watching can ever match a personal encounter with these great whales. It doesn't matter whether you're on a sailboat in Hawaii, or a larger motorboat in the north. Whether you take a

3-hour trip or a weeklong cruise, there is always excitement and emotion when spotting humpbacks.

In the tropics, you might see courting groups traveling at high speed or mothers and tiny calves. Because most boats to breeding areas are equipped with hydrophones, you may even get to hear a male singing, live. In the north you are often privileged to watch the whales feeding, breaching, and blowing high into the cold air.

No one who cares about wildlife could ever tire of these magnificent creatures, the humpbacks. The whaling days are gone – forever, we hope. But other man-made dangers remain that directly threaten humpbacks and their environment. Certain fishing techniques can have serious consequences. In recent years, humpbacks have become entangled in gillnets set across their feeding grounds in Newfoundland and New England. Chemical pollution, dumping of toxic waste, and dredging of shallow bays and banks may also adversely affect whales and their food sources.

If we've learned anything in the last few decades, it's this. Protecting the ocean in which humpbacks live is just as important to their survival as protecting the whales themselves.

WATCHING HUMPBACKS OFF HAWAII HAS BECOME A TRADITION. IN ORDER TO AVOID DISTURBING THE ANIMALS, VESSELS MUST STAY AT RESPECTFUL DISTANCES. TO HUMPBACKS, THE SHALLOW WATERS BETWEEN MAUI AND SEVERAL OTHER HAWAIIAN ISLANDS ARE ATTRACTIVE AS BREEDING GROUNDS. BREEDING SEASON OFFERS AN EXCELLENT CHANCE FOR WHALE-WATCHERS TO SEE COURTING GROUPS AND OTHER EXUBERANT DISPLAYS.

Can you hum along with the humpbacks? Below is theme C from the musical score of a whale song. Its highs, lows, and rhythms are punctuated with rests, just as human music is. Humpback males can send their mighty songs across five miles of ocean.

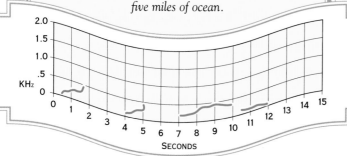

ABOUT
THE AUTHOR/PHOTOGRAPHER

François Gohier met his first humpback whale in Prince William Sound in 1976. Since then, he has observed and photographed them throughout the world. For nearly 20 years, his nature photography has graced numerous U.S. and European magazines, calendars, posters, and books. His credits include *National Geographic* and *GEO*. Although François' versatility is evident in the work he has done on birds, mammals, and other terrestrial subjects, he has concentrated on marine life the past few years. This is his second book on whales for Blake Publishing.

SPECIAL THANKS

For reviewing the manuscript and for numerous helpful contributions and suggestions, the writer-photographer wishes to thank:
✦ **Jeff Jacobsen,** Arcata, California
✦ **Dr. Charles Jurasz,** Sea Reach Ltd., Juneau, Alaska
✦ **Mason T. Weinrich,** Director, Cetacean Research Unit, Gloucester, Massachusetts
✦ **Mario A. Salinas Zacarias,** Universidad Autónoma de México
The writer-photographer is also indebted to:
✦ **Capt. Fred Douglass, Beryl Douglass,** and **Capt. Jim Douglass,** Cape Ann Whale Watching, Gloucester, Massachusetts
✦ **Paul Henry Forestell,** Pacific Whale Foundation, Kihei, Hawaii
✦ **Jason Lane,** Beachcomb Alaska, Angoon, Alaska and **Paul Johnson; Jean Riederer; Dr. Joseph Riederer; Marion Rider; Howard Rider; Mark Schilling;** and **Carolyn Gohier.**

GOOD BOOKS
& HELPING ORGANIZATIONS

✓ *Hawaii's Humpback Whales,* G. Kaufman & P. Forestell (Pacific Whale Foundation Press 1986).
✓ *The Sierra Club Handbook of Whales and Dolphins,* S. Leatherwood & R. Reeves (Sierra Club Books 1983).

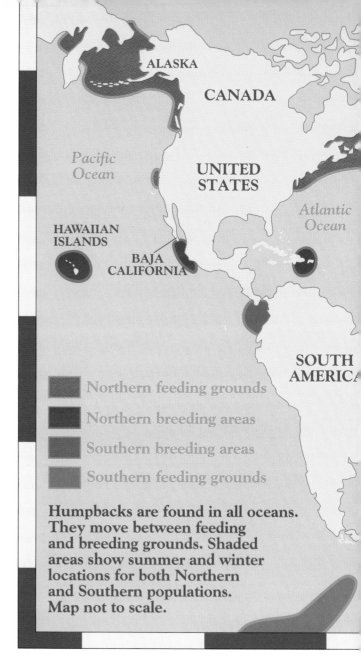

Northern feeding grounds
Northern breeding areas
Southern breeding areas
Southern feeding grounds

Humpbacks are found in all oceans. They move between feeding and breeding grounds. Shaded areas show summer and winter locations for both Northern and Southern populations. Map not to scale.

✓ *Observations: the Humpback Whales of Stellwagen Bank,* M. Weinrich (Whale Research Press 1985).
✓ **American Cetacean Society,** P.O. Box 2639, San Pedro, California 90731. Phone: (213) 548-6279.
✓ **Pacific Whale Foundation,** P.O. Box 1038, Kihei, Hawaii 96753. Phone: (808) 879-8811.
✓ **Oceanic Society Expeditions,** Ft. Mason Center, Bldg E, San Francisco, California 94123. Phone: (415) 441-1104.

WHERE TO WATCH HUMPBACKS

Humpbacks can be watched from shore in many places, but the most exciting viewing is usually from the water. Boat charters operate seasonally in many

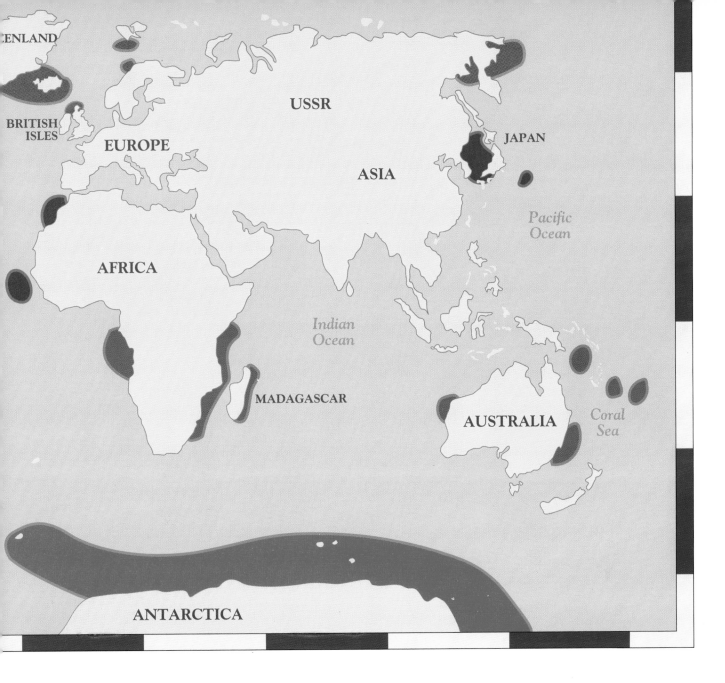

ENLAND

BRITISH
ISLES

EUROPE

USSR

ASIA

JAPAN

Pacific
Ocean

AFRICA

Indian
Ocean

MADAGASCAR

AUSTRALIA

Coral
Sea

ANTARCTICA

areas; some are sponsored by non-profit groups. The following is a partial list of locations; best sites are marked with a ✦

UNITED STATES:

✦ **Alaska:** summer viewing throughout Central and Southeast Alaska. Prince William Sound and Glacier Bay National Park are excellent. Numerous tour operators and excursions from Juneau, Gustavus, and other towns. One to 10-day tours, using sea kayaks to 45-foot boats.

California: summer viewing off central coast; most excursion activity out of San Francisco.

✦ **Hawaii:** winter viewing. Most excursion activity from Lahaina, Maui; some shore viewing from Kauai, Lanai, and Kona coast of Hawaii.

✦ **New England:** April through October, excellent viewing and daily excursions from numerous ports in Maine, Massachusetts, and New Hampshire.

CANADA:

✦ **Nova Scotia, New Brunswick, Newfoundland, Quebec.**

British Columbia: sporadic viewing around Vancouver Island.

ELSEWHERE:

✦ **Baja California,** Mexico: especially Los Cabos area at southern end of Sea of Cortez. Sporadic viewing along Mexican coast near **Puerto Vallarta.**

Dominican Republic; Puerto Rico; Bermuda; West Indies; and viewing on west and east coasts of **Australia.**

Call or write for other books in our growing nature series:

Habitats:
Tidepools ❖ The Kelp Forest ❖ Icebergs & Glaciers
Tropical Rainforests ❖ Coral Reefs ❖ The Desert

Marine Life:
A Raft of Sea Otters ❖ Seals & Sea Lions
A Pod of Gray Whales ❖ A Pod of Killer Whales
Humpback Whales ❖ Sharks ❖ Dolphins

Bird Life:
Hawks, Owls & Other Birds of Prey
Parrots, Macaws & Cockatoos
A Dazzle of Hummingbirds

SILVER BURDETT PRESS

© 1995 Silver Burdett Press
Published by Silver Burdett Press.
A Simon & Schuster Company
299 Jefferson Road,
Parsippany, NJ 07054
Printed in the United States of America